Julia Ward Howe

Modern society by Julia Ward Hove

Julia Ward Howe

Modern society by Julia Ward Hove

ISBN/EAN: 9783743331389

Manufactured in Europe, USA, Canada, Australia, Japa

Cover: Foto ©Lupo / pixelio.de

Manufactured and distributed by brebook publishing software
(www.brebook.com)

Julia Ward Howe

Modern society by Julia Ward Hove

BY

JULIA WARD HOWE.

BOSTON:

ROBERTS BROTHERS.

1881.

CONTENTS

MODERN SOCIETY.

———◆———

WHAT means this summons, oh friends! to the
groves of Academe? I heard, in the distance, the
measured tread of Philosophy. I mused: "How
grave and deliberate is she! How she matches
thought with thought! How patiently she questions inference and conclusion! No irrelevance,
no empty ballooning, is·allowed in that Concord
school. Nothing frivolous need apply there for
admission." And lo! in the midst of this severe
entertainment an interlude is called for in the
great theatre. The stage manager says, "Ring
up Puck. Wanted, an Ariel." And no Shake-
speare being at hand, I, of the sex much reproved
for never having produced one, am invited to fly
hither as well as my age and infirmities will allow,
and to represent to you that airy presence whose
folly, seen from the clouds, is wisdom; that presence which, changing with the changes of the year

and of the day, may yet sing, equally with the
steadfast stars and systematic planets, —

" The hand that made me is divine."

Modern society, concerning which you have bid
me discourse to you, is this tricksy spirit, many-
featured and many-gestured, coming in a question-
able shape, and bringing with it airs from heaven
and blasts from hell. I have spoken to it, and it
has shown me my father's ghost. How shall I
speak of it, and tell you what it has taught me?
You must think my alembic a nice one indeed,
since you bid me to the analysis of those subtle
and finely mingled forces. You have sent for me,
perhaps, to receive a lesson instead of giving one.
You may intend that, having tried and failed in
this task, I shall learn, for the future, the difficult
lesson of holding my peace. For so benevolent,
so disinterested an intention, I may have more
occasion to thank you beforehand, than you shall
find to thank me, having heard me.

But, since a text is supposed to make it sure
that the sermon shall have in it one good sentence,
let me take for my text a saying of the philosopher Kant, who, in one of his treatises, rests
much upon the distinction to be made between

logical and real or substantial opposition. According to him, a logical opposition is brought in view when one attribute of a certain thing is at once affirmed and denied. The statement of a body which should be at once stationary and in motion would imply such a contradiction, of which the result will be *nihil negativum irrepræsentabile.*

A real or substantial opposition is found where two contradictory predicates are recognized as coexistent in the same subject. A body impelled in one direction by a given force, and in another by its opposite, is easily cogitable. One force neutralizes the other, but the result is something, viz., rest. Let us keep in mind this distinction between opposites which exclude each other, and opposites which can coexist, while we glance at the contradictions of all society, ancient as well as modern.

How self-contradictory, in the first place, is the nature of man! How sociable he is! also how unsociable! We have among animals the gregarious and the solitary. But man is of all animals at once the most gregarious and the most solitary. This is the first and most universal contradiction, that of which you find at least the indication in every individual. But let us look for a moment at the contrasts which make one individual so unlike to another. We sometimes find it hard to believe the saying that God hath made of one blood all the nations of the earth. This in view of the contrast between savage and civilized nations, or between nations whose habits and beliefs differ one from the other. In the same race, in the same family also, we shall find the unlikeness which seems to set the bond of nature at defiance.

See this sly priest, bland and benevolent in proportion to the narrow limits of the minds which he controls. He hears the shrift of the brigand and assassin, of the girl mastered by passion, of the unfaithful wife and avenging husband. He gives an admonition, perhaps a grave one. He inflicts a penance, light or severe. He does not trust his penitents with the secret which can heal the plague-sores of humanity, — the secret of its moral power. But see the meek flock who come to him. See the whole range of consciences which cannot rest without his dismissing *fiat.* The rugged peasant drops on his knees beside the confessional. His horny palm relinquishes, without hesitation, the coin upon which it has scarcely closed. Or here alights from her carriage some woman of the world, bright in silks and jewels.

With a hush and a rustle, reaching the lowly bench, she, too, drops down, rehearses her wrong-doing, promises such reparation as is enjoined, and asks for the word of peace. Now this confessor, and one or more of his penitents, may be the children of the same father and mother, and yet they shall be as unlike in attitude and in character as two human beings can be. In the closest alliance of blood you may thus find the opposite poles of one humanity.

Humanity is, then, a thing of oppositions, and of oppositions which are polar and substantial. Its contradictions do not exclude, but, on the contrary, complement each other, and the action and reaction of these contradictions result in the mighty agreements of the State and of the Church, the intense sympathies and antipathies which bind or sunder individuals, the affections and disaffections of the family.

The opposite extremes of human nature embrace, between them, a wonderful breadth and scope. The correlation and coaction of this multitude of opposing forces on the wide arena of the world naturally give rise to a series of manifestations, voluntary and involuntary, changeful in form and color as a phantasmagoria, fitful as a fever-dream, but steadfast and substantial in the infinite science, out of which all things come. The unity in this web of contradictions is its great wonder. How if this unity prove to be the law of which the oppositions are but one clause? How if the perfect unity were only attainable through the freedom of the natural diversity? And what is the substance and sum of this fundamental agreement? The desire of good, the progressive conception of which marks, more than anything else, the progress of the race. We cannot tell out of what dynamics comes the initial of this fruitful and productive opposition. It is, perhaps, the very unity of the object which develops the diversity of action. In the progress of human society the diversity becomes constantly multiplied. Is the sense of the unity lost in consequence? No, it grows constantly with the growth of this opposing fact. As education is enlarged, as freedom becomes more general and entire, the agreement of mankind becomes greater in the objects to be attained for the promotion of their best interests.

We can suppose a family cast upon a barren shore, or forced to sit down in the midst of an uninhabited region. All of its members will wish to secure the necessary conditions of life, such as food, fuel, shelter, safety from destructive agencies. If left to themselves, one will naturally bestir himself to find fish, game, or fruits; another will bring in firewood; a third will plan a tent or hut; a fourth will stand sentry against any possible alarm. So a camp is a world in miniature; and if food and drink be plenty, and there be time to think of recreation, some one will carve a pipe from reed or willow, and, in answer to the piping, will come the dance. Or, if our pilgrims are too mystic and solemn for this, hymns will be sung, and the voice of prayer will lift the soul out of the poverty of its surroundings into that realm of imagination whose wealth far exceeds that of Ormus or of Ind.

I seem to hear at this point the *non placet* of those who ask for one thing and receive another. I was not sent for to philosophize, but to represent; and, with regard to the former process, "how not to do it" should have been my study. Modern society is my theme. Where shall I find society for you? Henry Thoreau found it here, in the passionless face of Nature. Here, the shy Hawthorne could dwell unmolested, not even overshadowed by the revered sage who makes reserve and distance such important elements of good manners. Mr. Alcott has transplanted here those olives whose sacred chrism rests upon his honored brow. The society which my words shall introduce here must be neither vulgar nor dull.

Now, if I had a flying-machine! Well, I have one, and its name is Memory. Sit with me, upon its movable platform, and I will give you some peeps at the thing itself, leaving you to discuss after me its *raison d'être*, its right to be. In experimental analysis, specimens are always exhibited. Let us look at modern society in Cairo, Shepherd's hotel, and the omnibus that bears one thither. The *table d'hôte* unites a catalogue as various as that of Don Giovanni. Here sit Sir Samuel and Lady Baker, famous as African explorers. You may all know something of the entertaining volumes which chronicle their discoveries and adventures. Lady Baker wears, at times, a necklace made of tiger's claws. Her husband shot the tiger in the great wilds of Africa, she loading the gun with which he did it.

She is Roumanian by birth, English by adoption, fair and comely. Sir Samuel is a burly Briton. They have with them a young African servant, dark and under-sized, with wild, crimped hair. Sir Samuel tells me that this is altogether the best human creature he ever knew. Lady Baker does not resent the extreme statement. I sit at table between a Russian count and an English baronet. The Russian and his two daughters are amiable and simple people. The baronet is a stanch Tory, as you will think natural when you hear his story. He was once a poor boy, hard at work in a coal mine. He used to walk six or seven miles daily, after working hours, in order to acquaint himself with those three Fates who are familiarly called the three R's. Becoming an expert in the coal business, he went through the upward grades of his profession, became a large owner of mines, and has now a heavy contract for supplying the Egyptian government with coal. He is a member of Parliament; and, when I saw him, was ready to start homeward on the first news of a division in the House. It was lately stated in a London paper that Lord Beaconsfield would probably raise him to the peerage before his own retirement from office. So, it may have been done by this time.

My Russian neighbors are much troubled about the fate of a poor Italian family whose chief has lost his occupation, and which is thus reduced to the extreme of want. "Why not get up a sub-scription at this hotel?" say I. They are very willing that I should. I draw up a paper, we sign our names and contributions. Sir George snubs us dreadfully, but gives us a sovereign. Sir Samuel snubs, and gives nothing. The necessary sum of money is raised, and the family is sent to its own country. Here, you see, are Russia, England, and America, combining, on Egyptian soil, to save Italy. This strange mixture is characteristic of the medley of the time.

We will not move yet, for the panorama of the table will save us that trouble. Here is one of the recognized beauties of London society. A very pretty woman, with dewy eyes, pearly teeth, dark, glossy hair, and a soft, fresh complexion. A French wardrobe sets off those natural advantages, with its happy disguises and apposite revelations. But it is not good for beauty that it should become a profession. This lady's fine eyes and teeth are made to do duty with such evident persistence of intention, that one absolutely dreads to see the glitter of the one and the flash of the other in the gymnastic of an advertised flirtation.

I cannot yet release you. Here are two gentlemen who wear the *tarbouche* with their European

costume. They were rebels in our war of secession,
and at its close took service with the Khedive.
Ignoring ancient sectional differences, they are
very cordial with us, their countrywomen. They
would be glad to see their country again, but
cannot get their salaries paid, the French and
English commissioners having taken the direction
of Egyptian finances, and making no allowance
for the past services of these American officers,
who were dismissed at their instance.

We are still at Shepherd's *table d'hôte*, and
before us sit an English nobleman and his wife,
who have obtained permission to give a *fête* at
the Pyramids. A gay party of English residents
and visitors are gathering to accompany them,
and presently the carriages and cavalcade start,
with a band of music, and a small army of ser-
vants. They illuminate the Great Pyramid with
colored fires, race their horses and donkeys through
the desert, sup and sleep in the Khedive's *kiosk*,
not without much boisterous mirth and disturb-
ance.

Or, behold me on Bairam day, paying a New-
Year's visit to the harem of the Khedive. A row
of grinning eunuchs, black as night, guard the
entrance. After various turns of ceremonial, we

greet the three princesses, all wives of the Khe-dive, who has many others not of this rank. In order not to give offence, we are obliged to smoke the *chibouque*, a pipe about five feet in length. We smile and courtesy at the proper moment, but find conversation difficult. They are curious to hear where we came from, and whither we are going. I ask whether they, also, enjoy travelling, and am reminded that their institutions do not allow it. These poor princesses little knew that in two months from that time an involuntary jour-ney awaited them, on the occasion of the Khe-dive's abdication, and departure from the country.

We please ourselves, in these days, with the praise of Islamism, and think, quite rightly, that Mahomet and his Koran had their *raison d'être*, and have done their part for mankind. But here is Islamism in modern society. The howling der-vishes sit on the ground groaning *Allah, Allah.* By and by they rise, and bend their heads back-ward and forward until the most eminent among them fall in fits, and are taken up in an unhappy condition. Within a short distance from our hotel, we hear of a company of men met for a religious exercise. One of them chews a glass goblet and swallows it. Another endeavors to swallow a small snake. A third gashes himself wildly with a sword. These are religious enthusiasts. If their faith be genuine, these dangerous experiments, they say, can do them no harm.

These things remind us of the temptation of Christ: "If thou be the Son of God, cast thyself down from hence."

But let us leave the city and hotel, and betake ourselves to the historic river, dumb with all its mouths, and poor with all its wealth. Modern society is well represented on board our steamer. Here are two Californian gentlemen, two sons of a Sandwich Island missionary, two or three Italians. Here is a sister-in-law of John Bright. She has visited Alaska, and considers this Nile trip a small parenthesis in her voyage round the world. Here are an English couple, belonging to fashionable life. Here is a clergyman of the same nation, who glories in the fact that Dr. Johnson hated, or said he hated, a Whig. Here is an American who cannot visit the ruins because his whole day is divided into so many glasses of milk, to be taken at such and such times.

We land one day at Assiout, and visit its bazaars. The trade in ostrich feathers is brisk, the natives steadily raising their prices as the demand in-

2

creases, until we find that the feathers might be more cheaply bought in London or Paris. Amid the general confusion of tongues I am accosted by a handsome youth, cleanly and civil, who speaks fair English, and asks if he can serve me.

Who are you? A pupil of the American Mission School in this place. He brings two of his fellow-pupils to speak with me. One of these is a girl, whose innocent, uncovered face seems to rebuke the hidden faces of the Arab women, veiled and disfigured to evince their modesty, but making more evident the immodesty of the men.

We return to our steamer, followed by a crowd of boys and girls, shrieking and naked, who plunge into the water to get the *backshish,* which some of our party throw them. On the bank stand two beautiful youths, nearly black, with eyes like sloes, and with crisped hair standing erect like a flame above their foreheads. They are clad in kilts of white cotton cloth. Struck with their beauty, we inquire of what tribe they are. "Of the Bischouri," says our dragoman, "a tribe of the desert, who feed only upon uncooked grain." To the last their bright smile pursues us with its pathos. Would that they, too, were pupils of the

American Mission School. Would not our vegetarian chief send for them ?*

We gallop across the sands to a point opposite
Philæ, and reach the sacred spot by boat. We
picnic among its tombs, climb its *pylon*, and
remark upon the beauty of the view. At the
first cataract, which is very near this place, an
Arab woman shows me her baby with the pride
of Eve or Queen Victoria. It has a nose-ring
of brass wire, and similar adornments in the top
of each ear. On my way back to the boat, my
pocket is picked by a cunning youth. The Arabs
of the desert will compare in this respect with
the Arabs of European streets. A little Arab
girl offers to sell me her rag doll, whose veil is
bedizened with spangles. A little water-carrier,
proud of her English, says, " Lady, give me backshish."

This shall end my peep at modern society in
Egypt.

But one more personal remembrance you must
accord me. The scene is a dirty, muddy street in
a Cyprus seaport. The time is not far from noon.
I am exploring, with some curiosity, the new jewel

* Mr. Alcott, Dean of the Concord School of Philosophy, has
always been known as a vegetarian.

which Lord Beaconsfield has added to the crown of Great Britain.

What a mean, poor bazaar is this ; what dull streets, what a barren place to live in, especially since *methymenic* Albion has drunk up all the best of the wine! I pass a shop, and a bright presence beams out upon me. It is Lady Baker, with her fair, luminous face, full of energy and resource. Sir Samuel, she tells me, is in the back shop buying hardware for a hard journey. For they intend to travel through the island in a huge covered wagon, drawn by oxen, which will be to them at once vehicle and hotel. Where they went, and how they fared, I know not, nor would it here import us, if I did. I only mention the appearance of these friends in this place, because this appearance was so characteristic of modern society, and because so many of its elements appeared there in their persons. The education and high society of England, the court, the literary circles, the almighty publisher, for an intended volume was surely looming in the foreground of their picture. And here I have clearly got hold of one feature of modern society ; this is, that everything is everywhere. The Zulus are in London, the Londoners in Zululand. Empress Eugenie, the exploded star of French fashion in its highest supremacy, visits Cape Town. The stars and stripes protect American professors on the shores of the Bosphorus, within view of Mount Lebanon. It would not surprise us to learn that a party of our countrymen had read the Declaration of Independence beside the Pools of Solomon, or within the desolate heart of Moab.

In Jaffa of the Crusaders, Joppa of Peter and Paul, I find an American Mission School, kept by a worthy lady from Rhode Island. Prominent among its points of discipline is the clean-washed face which is so enthroned in the prejudices of Western civilization. One of her scholars, a youth of unusual intelligence, finding himself clean, observes himself to be in strong contrast with his mother's hovel, in which filth is just kept clear of fever point. " Why this dirt ?" quoth he ; "that which has made me clean, will cleanse this also." So without more ado, the process of scrubbing is applied to the floor, without regard to the danger of so great a novelty. This simple fact has its own significance, for if the innovation of soap and water can find its way to a Jaffa hut, where can the ancient, respectable, conservative dirt-devil feel himself secure ?

The maxim also becomes vain nowadays, that there should be a place for everything, and that everything should be in its place. Cleopatra's Needles point their moral in London and in New York. The Prince of Wales hunts tigers in the Punjaub. Hyde Park is in the desert or on the Nile. America is all over the world. Against this universal game of "Puss in the Corner," reaction must come, some day, in some shape, or anywhere will mean nowhere, for those who, starting in the geographical pursuit of pleasure, fail to find it and never return home.

The oppositions of humanity have undergone many changes. Paul characterized them in his day as "Greek and Barbarian, bond and free, male and female." Christianity effaced old oppositions and created new ones. The old oppositions were national, personal, selfish. The new opposition was moral. It struck at evils, not at men, and tended to unite the latter in a patient and reasonable overcoming of the former. I know that the white heat at which its first blow was dealt left much for philosophy to elaborate, for science to adjust and apply. A Jesus, arrived at the plenitude of his intellectual vigor, could only have three years in which to formulate his weighty doctrine, and could not have had these without much care and hindrance. His work lay in the normal direction of human nature. In spite of lapses and relapses, mankind slowly creep towards the great unification which will make the savage animals and the selfish passions the only enemies of the human race. Modern society rests upon this unification as its basis of action. A positive philosophy which Auguste Comte did not elaborate absorbs its highest thought, and dictates its largest measures.

And so prophetic souls bid farewell to the old negations. In their view, the lion is already reconciled to the lamb. The taming of the elements prefigures the general reconciliation. The deadly lightning runs on errands and carries messages. The Titan steam is the servant of commerce and industry, meek as Hercules when armed with the distaff of Omphale. Emulation, the desire to excel, exquisite, dangerous stimulant to exertion, is not in our day educated to the intensification of self, but to the enlargement of public spirit and of general interest. The constant discoveries of new treasures in our material world, of gold, silver, iron, and copper, of states to be built up and of harvests to be sown and reaped,

are accompanied by corresponding discoveries concerning the variety of human gifts and their application to useful ends.   What men and women can
be good for may be more voluminously stated
to-day than in any preceding age of the world's
history.

Comparison should be a strong point in modern
society.   When travelling was laborious and difficult, the masses of one country knew little concerning those of another.   When learning was
rare, and instruction costly and insufficient, the
few knew the secrets of thought and science, the
many not even knowing that such things were to
be known.   When wealth was uncommon, luxury
was monopolized by a small class, the greater part
of mankind earning only for themselves the right
to live poorly.   When distinctions were absolute,
low life knew nothing of high life but what the
novelist could invent, or the servant reveal.   How
changed is all this to-day !   Competence, travel,
tuition, and intelligent company are within the
reach of all who will give themselves the trouble
to attain them.   The first consequence of this is
that we become able to make the largest and most
general comparison of human conditions which
has ever been possible to humanity, nor does this

ability regard the present alone. The unveiling of the treasures of the past, the interpretation of its experience and doctrine which we owe to the scholar and archæologist, enable us to compare remote antiquity with the things of the last minute. The work of antiquarian science culminates in the discovery of the prehistoric man. Theology had long before invented the post-historic angel. Now, indeed, we ought to be able to choose the best out of the best, since the whole is laid in order before us. But the chronic trouble* hangs upon us still. Had we but such wisdom to choose as we have chance to see! The gifts of our future are still shown us in sealed caskets. Which of these conceals the condition of our true happiness? The leaden one, surely, of which we distrust the dull exterior, trusting in the inner brightness which it covers.

What is the problem of modern society?

How to use its vast resources. Here is where the office of true ethic comes in. No gift can make rich those who are poor in wisdom. The wealth which should build up society will pull it down if its possession lead to fatal luxury and indulgence. The freedom of intercourse which makes one nation known to another, and puts the

culture of the most advanced at the service of the
most barbarous, is like a flood which carries everywhere the seeds of good and of evil. The ripen-
ing of these depends much upon the accident of
the human soil they may happen to find. But
careful husbandry will have even more to do with
the result.

To America it was said at the outset, " Pre-
pare to receive the World, and to make it free."
Oh, World, so full of corruption and of slavery,
wilt thou not rather bind us with thy gangrenous
fetters ? Wilt not the wail of thy old injustice and
suffering prolong itself until the new strophe of
hope shall be lost and forgotten ?

Where is God's image in this human brute who
lands on our shores, full only of the insolence of
beggary ? Far, far be from us ever the methods
and procedures which have made or left him what
he is. Honor and glory to those patient, good men
and women who will redeem his children from the
degradation which seems almost proper to him.
Theirs be a crown above that of the poet or
orator !

Modern society, then, is chiefly occupied with a
vast assimilation of novelties. This task is by no
means imposed upon us alone. While the New

World has to digest races and traditions, the Old World has to digest ideas. Thanks to the good Puritan stomach which we inherit, the process goes on here, with little interruption. But across the seas, in Rome, in Germany, in Russia, what nausea, what quarrelling with the fatal morsel upon which Providence compels the lips to close!

"*Non possumus!*" say the priests of the old order. "*Possum,*" replies the eternal power. The French republic and the English monarchy succeed best in this altering of old habits to suit new emergencies. But where extremes are greatest, the contest is naturally fiercest. A Pope fears the cup of poisoned chocolate, and dares not drink the wine of the eucharist without a taster; the throne of the Russian autocrat is over the deadly mine of the Nihilist. German vanity and diplomacy bring back the shadow of the mediæval muddle. The living heart's blood of humanity comes to us out of these struggles, an immeasurable gift, for good or for evil. Can we be quick enough with our schools, just enough in our government, sincere and devout enough in our churches? What will Europe do with the ideas? What will America do with the people? These are the questions of the present time.

One of the serious social questions of the day is the omnipotence of money. People often use this expression in a *quasi* sarcastic sense, not seriously intending what they say. But the power of money nowadays is such that it becomes us seriously to ask whether there is anything that it cannot do. What ancient strongholds of taste, sentiment, and prejudice has it not stormed and carried?

A servant, who sought a place during the first years of the shoddy inflation, asked a lady who was willing to engage her, "Are you shoddy, ma'am, or old family? I want to live with shoddy, because it pays the highest wages." The watchwords of society as often come from its humbler as from its higher level, and this woman unconsciously uttered the word which was to rule society from that time to this. Money, during the last twenty years, has swept over most of the old landmarks, and obliterated them.

Religion itself stands aghast at this baptism of gold, which can convert the alien and the heathen, ay, the brigand and the robber, into saints of social prestige. For money bribes the court and pulpit, and buys the press; the highest rank, the highest genius, pay homage to it. If the duke has not money, he will seek in wedlock the most undesirable of women, if she be also the richest. Royalty bows to the splendid cloak of vulgarity, and invites it to dine and drive. Happy day, you will say, for labor, which money symbolizes. Monarchs may well show it respect. But money does not always symbolize honest and intelligent industry. A great fortune often represents transactions akin to theft; sometimes the thing itself, which the world is Spartan enough to approve of, if the criminal can only escape positive detection. Those, too, who have earned their money honestly, leave it to children who turn their back upon the class of which their parents came, and desire to know nothing of the bread-winning arts which they were constrained to practise.

We have had, within the last ten years, a severe lesson concerning the instability of wealth in some of its most trusted forms. Yet are we not compelled by sympathy and antipathy, at the bottom of our hearts, to pay it an homage which our lips would not avow? Do we not desire wealth for our children as the condition which shall set our minds at rest concerning them? When we see mediocrity and vulgarity riding in the swift carriage, and wearing the jewels and the robes, bright in everybody's eyes and praised in everybody's mouth, do we not harbor somewhere a regret that we have not, in some way possible to us, set our best abilities to work to secure a similar distinction for ourselves?

It should not frighten one to see the court and its underlings venal. Court and courtiers are a show, and money is the condition by which a show lives. But I look into the domain of letters, and ask whether that is still uncorrupted. I do not think that it is. The refined tastes of literary people lead them to value entertainment at the hands of the rich. The luxurious rooms, the abundant table, the easy *persiflage* in which worldly tact knows enough to flatter recognized talent. Do not these *illicebræ* seduce, to-day, even the stern heart of philosophy?

How unkind was society to Margaret Fuller! It was reluctant to show her the courtesy due to a gentlewoman. Its mean gossip treated her as if she had been beyond the pale of elegance and good taste, verging away even from good behavior. What was her offence against society? A humanity too large and absorbing, a mind too brave and independent for its commonplace. Add to these the fact that she had neither fashion nor fortune.

The things she asked for are granted to-day by every thinking mind, and she is remembered as illustrious. But if she could come back to-morrow as she was, poor in purse and plain in person, and assume her old leadership, would Boston treat her any better than it did in days of yore? Would she not find, even among Brook farmers, a looking toward Beacon Street which might surprise her? The literary man, who went so bravely from abstract philosophy to its concrete expression, whose learned hands took up the spade and hoe, and whose early peas were praised by those who contemned his principles, would he, at a later day, — grown urbane and fashionable, — would he have bowed without a pang to his former self, if he had met him, dusty and on foot, in Central Park, he himself being well mounted?

I said just now that money could buy the press. This is shameful, because the press, more than any other power, can afford to be frank and sincere. Freedom is the very breath of life in its nostrils, yet is it to-day largely salaried by the enemies of freedom. While speaking of the press, I will mention the regret with which I lately read, in the "Boston Daily Advertiser," an editorial treating of the expulsion of the Jesuits from France.

The writer, who denounced this measure with some severity, described the religious body with which it deals as a band of mild and inoffensive men, chiefly occupied with the tuition of youth. He might as well have characterized a tiger as a harmless creature, incapable of the use of fire-arms.

To me the worship of wealth means, in the present, the crowning of low merit with undeserved honor, — the setting of successful villany above unsuccessful virtue.   It means absolute neglect and isolation for the few who follow a high heart's love through want and pain, through evil and good report.   It means the bringing of all human resources, material and intellectual, to one dead level of brilliant exhibition — a second Field of the Cloth of Gold — to show that the barbaric love of splendor still lives in man, with the thirst for blood, and other *quasi* animal passions. It means, in the future, some such sad downfall as Spain had when the gold and silver of America had gorged her soldiers and nobles; something like what France experienced after Louis XIV. and XV.   I am no prophet, and, least of all, a prophet of evil; but where, oh where, shall we find the antidote to this metallic poison?   Perhaps in the homœopathic principle of cure. When the money miracle shall be complete, when the gold Midas shall have turned everything to gold, then the human heart will cry for flesh and blood, for brain and muscles. Then shall manhood be at a premium, and money at a discount.

The French have found, among many others, one fortunate expression. They speak of a life of representation, by which they mean the life of a person conspicuous in the great world. This society of representation has some recognition in every stage of civilization, since even nations which we consider barbarous have their festivals and processions. The ministerial balls in Paris, and perhaps many other entertainments in that city, are of this character.

The guests are admitted in virtue of a card, which is really a ticket, though money cannot command it. Many of the persons entertained are not personally acquainted with either host or hostess, and do not necessarily make their acquaintance by going to their house. Everything is arranged with a view to large effects: music, decorations, supper, etc. A party of friends may go there for their own amusement, or a single individual for his own. But there are no general introductions given, there is no social fusion.

Now this I call society of representation. It
bears about the same relation to genuine society
that scene-painting bears to a carefully finished
picture. People of culture and education enjoy
a peep at this spectacular drama of the social
stage, but their idea of society would be something very different from this. Where this show-
society monopolizes the resources of a community, it implies either a dearth of intellectual
resources, or a great misapprehension of what is
really delightful and profitable in social intercourse.

Where the stage form of society predominates
too largely, its intimate form languishes and
declines. The communings of a chosen few
around a table simply spread, with no view to
the recognition of the great Babylon, but rather
with a pleasure in its avoidance; refined sympathy and support given and received in a round
of daily duties, by those whose hands are busy
and whose minds are full; the inner sweetness
of a beautiful song or poem, the kindling of mind
from mind, till all become surprised at what each
can do, — this sort of society maintains itself by
keeping the noisy rush of the crowd at arm's
length. Horace says, —

" Odo profanum vulgus et arceo,"

and I, a democrat of the democrats, will say
so too. I reverence the masses of mankind, rich
or poor. My heart beats high when I think of
the good which human society has already
evolved, and of the greater good which is in
store for those who are to come after us. But
I hate the profane vulgarity which courts public
notice and mention as the chief end of existence,
and which, in so doing, puts out of sight those
various ends and interests which each generation
is bound to pursue for itself, and to promote for
its successors.

The time of poor Marie Antoinette was the cul-
mination of such a period of show. Its glare and
glitter, and its lavish waste, had put out of sight
the true and intimate relations of man to man.
And so, as the gilded portion of the age made its
musters of beautiful empty heads, of vanities
throned upon vanities, the ungilded part made
its deadly muster of discontent, displeasure, and
despair. The empty heads fell, and much that
was precious and noble fell with them. The
great stage produced its bloody drama, and the
curtain of horror closed upon it.

Critics of society usually direct their invective
against the extravagance and shallowness of this

exhibitory department, and would almost make these an excuse for the opposite. extreme of misanthropic spleen and avoidance. They should remember that while society, from an inward necessity, provides for these musterings and displays, it is unable to provide for that intimate and personal intercourse which individuals must found and cultivate for themselves. So much is left for each one of us to do, to find our peers, and open with them an honest exchange of our best for their best. The family most easily begins this, with its intense and ever-enlarging interests. Out of true family life comes a neighborhood ; out of a neighborhood the body politic, and the body sympathetic.

If, in the matter of social intercourse, show is allowed to usurp the place of substance, the indolence of mankind must bear its part of the blame. It is far easier to order a suit for the great occasion, than to brighten one's mental jewels for the small one. Many a soldier is brave on parade, who would not shine on a field of battle. Many a woman will pass for elegant in a ball-room, or even at a court drawing-room, whose want of true breeding would become evident in a chosen company.

The reason why education is usually so poor

among women of fashion is, that it is not needed for the life which they elect to lead. With a good figure, good clothes, and a handsome equipage, with a little reading of the daily papers, and of the fashionable reviews, and above all, with the happy tact which often enables women to make a large display of very small acquirements, the woman of fashion may never feel the need of true education. We pity her none the less, since she will never know its peace and delight.

In our own country, at this moment, and in Europe as well, ambitions seem to be unduly directed to this department of social action, the training and discipline for which differ widely from that proper to intimate and domestic life. Hence comes an observable regard, not to appearances only, but to appearance. As actors often paint their faces too highly for near effects, in order to look well at the farthest point of view, so the dress and manners of the day fit themselves for the stage of the great world, and their wearers seem to meditate not only what will not appear amiss, but what will attract attention by some singularity of becoming effect. Hence the supremacy for the time of those whose calling it is to minister to appearance. The tailor has

long been a man of destiny, but the modern plain-
ness of male attire has somewhat sobered his
pretensions. But look at the sublime arrogance
of the ladies' dressmaker, and the almost equally
sublime meekness of the victim, who not only
submits, but desires to be as wax in her hands.
This supreme functionary has, of course, *carte
blanche* for her ordinances. The subject says to
her, "Do what you will with me. Make me
modest or immodest. Tie up my feet or
straighten my arms till use of them becomes
impossible. Deprive my figure of all drapery,
or upholster it like a window-frame. Nay, set
me in the centre of a movable tent, but array me
so that people shall look at me, and shall say I
look well."

I cannot but hate, to-day, the slavish fashion
which seems to have been invented in order to
intensify that self-consciousness which is the
worst enemy of beauty. It is administered by
means of a system of lacets and whalebones,
which everywhere impinge upon nature. A
young lady who is in her dress like a sword in
its scabbard (the French name for the fashion
is *fourreau*), is made to think of this point, and
of that, until her whole gait and movement be-

come an interrogation of her silks and elastics. Can I sit? Can I walk? Can I put this foot forward, or lift this hand to my head? Ask the satin strait-jacket in which your artist has imprisoned you, receiving high compensation for the service. Much as I resent this constraint and restraint of the body, my saddest thought is, that where it is endured the mind has first been enslaved.

Foreign travel is so established a feature in American life, that it may well become us to take account of what it costs and comes to.

Our own importation of men and women is various and enormous. They who come to us poor and ignorant in one generation, are seen comfortable and well educated in the next. The disfranchised and landless man comes to us, and receives political rights, and the title of a farm in fee simple. No inordinate tribute robs him of the product of his industry, be it large or small. He pays to the State what it pays him well to afford, for protection and education. But how is it with the tribute which Europe levies upon us in the shape of our sons and daughters?

Many polite tastes have, no doubt, been fostered in our young men by studies pursued in a

German university, or art learned in a French studio. Some of the best scholars of the elder generation have profited, in their youth, by such advantages. But if we go beyond the limits of literary or professional life, we may not consider the results so fortunate. Our society-men sometimes become so depolarized in their tastes and feelings, as to be at ease nowhere but in Europe, and not much at ease there. Those who return bring back a love of betting and of horse-racing, and ape the display of European grandees as far as their fortunes will allow.

And our young women? Some of them study soberly abroad, and return to give their countenance and support to all that is improving and refining in their own country. Some float hither and thither, between England and Italy, like a feather on the wave, disappearing at last. The Daisy Millerish chit is seen, offending in pure ignorance of what common-sense should easily teach mothers and daughters.

Family groups of Americans are often met with in Europe, in which one figure is wanting. This is the father, absent, in America, working at his business or speculation. These ladies are often companionable people, who enjoy good hotels, galleries, music on the public square, and, above all, the sensation of being far from home.

. One feels about them a dreary atmosphere of homelessness. As the writer of the Potiphar papers, while watching a gay young mother's performance in the "German," was constrained to think of a complaining babe in her nursery, so, in hearing those ladies boast of their enjoyments, one cannot help remembering with commiseration the wifeless husband and daughterless father at home, who works like a steam-fan to keep these butter-flies in motion.

More sad still are my reflections, when I hear that numbers of American girls, with large or even moderate fortunes, go abroad and allow it to be known that they seek a husband with a title. These are to be had, of various grades, if the pecuniary consideration be only sufficient. And so many of our laborious men of business work hard in order to earn for themselves the luxury of a titled son-in-law, who has not the ability to earn his own support, and would scorn to do it if he had.

American women with money are at a premium in fashionable Europe. Even without this supreme merit, they are favorites. A London journal calls attention to the fact that some of the leading ladies in the fashionable London of to-day are Americans. The versatility of mind and ease of manner which a free and social life develops, appear in strong contrast with the results of the more formal education, which are often seen in the opposite extremes of timidity and assurance.

As our young men are often entrapped, while abroad, into marriages which prove to be very unwise and unsuitable, I wish very much that we might bring and keep our young people in a better understanding with each other, so that even the most ambitious among them should be content to marry with their peers, and abide in the home of their fathers.

I have been surprised, at some periods of my late visit to Europe, to perceive the growing interest of thinking people in all that is most·characteristic of American progress. Again and again, in private and in public, I have found myself invited to discourse concerning the happy country in which popular education has been so long established, that its results are no longer putative, but ascertained and verified. The country in which the fairest woman, provided she be a modest one, can walk abroad by day or night, unmolested and

unsuspected, the country in which women have
acquired the courage to think for themselves, and
to stand by each other.

These invitations, though not given in derision,
yet seemed akin to the Hebrew refrain, "Sing us
one of the songs of Zion!" And when I related
the facts familiar to all of us, to those who listened
with half-incredulous wonder, it was, indeed, like
singing the Lord's song of freedom in a strange
land.

The reasons why Europe should come to
America are obvious and pressing. The reasons
why America should visit Europe are equally
binding and cogent. The material and the moral
life of to-day are kept at their height by this flux
and reflux of human personality, which carries
with it every variety of opinion and experience.
Could we only send our best abroad, and for the
best reasons! Could Europe only send her best,
also, for their best help and study! But the
human average profits first of all by its material enlargement, and will be received just as
it is. So, our fools go abroad, to show that
folly is a thing of all times and climes; and,
along with the tidal wave of ignorance and big-
otry, the dark, designing Jesuit seeks our shore,

and spins his fatal web among our rose-trees.
Sun of divine truth, storms of divine justice,
sweep away the evil and ripen the good!

When I see an American of either sex caught
in the vortex of European attraction, depolarized
from natural relations, and charmed into alliance
with feudal barbarism and ignorance, my heart
rings the bell of alarm which is hung at the gates
of Paradise.

From all these Western splendors can this
shallow soul turn away? From these golden
fields whose overflow gives Europe food, while
her human overflow gives them labor? From this
large construction of human right, which lifts the
cruel yoke from the neck of labor, and gives him
who earns the livelihood of many his own life to
enjoy and perfect? From this holy record of pious
endeavor, from these splendid achievements of
souls inspired by freedom, thou canst go, joyous
and triumphant, to pay homage to the lies which
are no longer believed by those who profess them ;
lies whose fallacy America exposes every day and
hour to the detection of the world.

Thou wilt accept a title, empty as an egg-shell,
for a thing truly noble! Thou wilt call a courtier's grimace polite, a courtesan's fashion elegant!

Thou wilt curry favor in a vulgar court, courtesy-
ing low to a prince of harlequins and harlots!
Thou, child of the Puritans, wilt kneel and kiss
the hand which, still and sole, disputes with Christ
the mastery of the world! Then art thou simply
an anachronism! Some are born into the world
centuries before their time, some centuries after it.

Other attractions, innocent in themselves, and
conceivable to all, detain some of our valued fel-
low-citizens in perpetual exile. The quiet and
beauty of English country-life, the literary and
artistic resources of a foreign capital, the romances
of ancient chateaux and cathedrals, some delicious
touch of climate, some throbbing beauty of a south-
ern sky. How delightful we have found these,
it is as much a pain as a pleasure to remember!
But let us also call to mind the lesson of a well-
known fairy tale. While Beauty prolongs her
absence, the faithful Beast languishes and comes
nigh unto death. While we enjoy these choice
delights, the society to which we belong is sowing
its wheat and its tares. We are far from the field
in which the life of our own generation is planted
and tended. Every honest heart, every thinking
mind, has its value in the community to which it
belongs. Our value, such as it is, remains want-

ing to our community, and, when its crises of trial
shall come, we shall not have been trained by
watchful experience to understand either their
cause or their remedy.

How delightful was Italy to Milton! His Alle-
gro and Pensieroso show that he could fully appre-
ciate both its mirth and its majesty. He returns
not the less to live out a life of illustrious service
in his own country, where his brave heart and
philosophic mind were of more avail to his time
than even his sacred song to ours.

No one has any reason to be surprised at any
new manifestation of human folly. Yet I am
sometimes surprised, to-day, by the disrespect
which is often shown to the word "Protestant."
This name dates, at farthest, from the time of
Luther, but the fact for which it stands is as old
as human history. Moses made a protest when
he led his people out of the luxury and slavery
of Egypt to find the free hills of Judæa, and
to build on one of them a temple to the God
of freedom. Christ made His protest against
the hypocrisy and injustice of the old social
and ecclesiastical order. England and France
have made their protests against monarchical supremacy. Both went back from their daring deter-

mination, but the lesson was not forgotten. The Puritans made their protest when they faced the frowning sea and the savage wilderness, in order that they might train their children, and live themselves in the freedom which conscience asks. Mr. Garrison and his associates made their protest against American slavery. Mrs. Butler, of England, makes her protest to-day against the personal degradation of women. Lucy Stone makes hers against their political enslavement.

Does society inherit ? Is man the heir of man ? Whence come those creatures of the present day who smile, and shrug their shoulders, and feebly say, " We don't protest. Our fathers did something of the kind, upon what ground we cannot possibly imagine. But we are quite of another sort. We don't protest."

To those courageous souls which, alone and unaided, have been able to face the world's passion and inertia, — to those leaders of forlorn hopes who have seen glory in the depths of death and have sought it there, — to those voices proclaiming in the wilderness the triumphant progress of truth, — to those brave spirits whose strength the fires of hell have annealed, not consumed, — my soul shall ever render its glad and duteous homage. And if,

in my later age, I might seek the crowning honor
of my life, I should seek it with that small, faithful band who have no choice but to utter their
deepest conviction, and abide its issues.   Fruitful
shall be their pains and privations.   They who
have sown in tears the seeds of unpopular virtue,
shall reap its happy harvest in the good and grati-
tude of mankind.

CHANGES IN AMERICAN SOCIETY.

————◆————

I HAVE been invited to speak to you to-day concerning changes in American society. In preparing to consider this subject, I cannot but remember that the very question of social change is to some people an open one. The supposition of any real onward movement in society is as unwelcome and as untrue to these persons as was Galileo's theory concerning the revolution of the earth around the sun. They will assert, as indeed they may, that the same crimes are committed in all ages, with the same good deeds to counterbalance them and that the capital tendencies of human nature are always substantially the same. This also must be allowed. The error of these friends consists in overlooking the most characteristic and human of these tendencies, which is that of progressive desire. This trait, deeper and stronger than the mere love of change, pushes the whole

4

heterogeneous mass of humanity onward in a way from which there is no return.

The laws of human motive and action, meanwhile, remain as steadfast and immovable as the laws by whose application Galileo made his discovery. To discern at once the steadfast truth and its metamorphic developments will be the task of the greatest wisdom.

When Theodore Parker invited the religious world to consider the transient and the permanent elements of Christianity, he made a popular application of a truth long known to philosophy. This truth is that life in all of its aspects exhibits these two opposite qualities or conditions. Much is transient in the individual, more is permanent in the race.

The study of anthropology, so greatly enriched to-day by discovery and investigation, would give us much to say under both of these heads, but most, I think, under the last.

I remember that in reading Livy's history of the second Punic war, in our own war time, I was struck by certain resemblances between the time in which he wrote and that in which I read him. When I learned from his pages that the merchants and ship-owners of ancient Rome managed to impose the most worthless of their vessels upon the government for the transport of troops and provisions, I exclaimed, "What Yankees these Romans were!"

In reading some well-known satires of Horace I have been struck with the resemblance of the ancient to the modern bore. Boileau's famous take-off of the dinner given by a *parvenu* is scarcely more than a French adaptation of the feast of Nasidienus, as described by the Roman bard who was Boileau's model. .

In Virgil's account of the good housewife, who rises early in order to measure out the work of the household, and in Solomon's description of the thrifty woman of his time, one sees the value set upon feminine industry and economy in times far removed from our own, yet resembling it in this appreciation.

On the other hand, the dissimilarity of ancient and modern society is equally seen in the same mirror of literature. The mention of matters which, by common consent, are banished from decent speech to-day, the position of Woman, from the vestal virgin buried alive for breach of trust to the *devium scortum*, whom Horace frankly invites to his feast, the gross superstition which

saw in religion little save portents and propitia-
tion, — these mark on the dial of history an hour
as distant from our own in sympathy as in time.

You will wish to hear from me some account
of changes which have come within the sphere of
my own observation, both as I have been able to
see for myself, and to compare what I have seen
with what I have received from the generation
immediatly preceding my own. Let me remind
you that, with all the advantages of personal
observation, it may be more difficult for us to give
a true account of the age to which we belong
than of more distant times, upon which thought
and reflection have already done their critical
and explanatory work. Familiarity so dulls the
edge of perception, as to make us least acquainted
with things and persons making part of our daily
life. Mindful of these difficulties, I will do my
best to characterize the threescore years which
have carried me into and out of the heart of the
nineteenth century.

I have seen in this time a great growth in the
direction of liberal thought, of popular government,
of just laws and useful institutions. I have seen
human powers so multiplied by mechanical appli-
ances as to destroy the old measures of time and

distance, and almost to justify the veto once laid by the great Napoleon upon the use of the word "impossible": "*Ne me dîtes jamais ce bête de mot,*" said he; and it has now become more *bête* than ever.

What feature of society has not changed in the phantasmagoria of these wonderful lustres? Each decade has made a fool of the one which went before it. Whether in the region of extended observation and experiment, or in that of subtle and profound investigation, human effort has seemed in this time to put itself at compound interest, working at once with matters infinitely little and with matters infinitely great, and surely introducing mankind to a higher plane of comfort and co-operation than has been reached in anterior ages.

While the mechanism of life has thus been brought much nearer to perfection by the labor of our age, the principles of life remain such as they have always been.

Pile luxury as high as you will, health is better, and the body of a well-fed and not over-worked ploughman is, nine times out of ten, a better possession than the body of a man of fortune, especially if he be at the same time a man of pleasure.

Marshal and gild the pomp of circumstance, and do it homage with bated breath, character remains the true majesty, honor and intelligence its prime ministers. Money can help people to education, by paying for the support of those who can give it. But money cannot excuse its possessor from the smallest of the mental operations through which, if at all, a man comes to know what, as a man, he should know.

The great *desiderata* of humanity still remain these : to preserve the integrity of nature, the purity of sentiment, and the coherence of thought. The great extension of educational opportunities which we see to-day should make the attainment of these objects easier than in ages of less instruction. But while the pursuit of them is ever normal to the human race, the inherent difficulties of their attainment remain undiminished. Without self-dicipline and self-sacrifice, no man to-day attains true education, or the dignity of true manhood. For here comes in the terrible fact of man's freedom as a moral agent.

Could our age possess and administer the powers of the universe to its heart's content, in that heart would yet rest the issues of its life and of its death.

The period of which I have to speak has certainly witnessed great improvements in the theory of hygiene. The old heroic treatment of diseases has nearly disappeared. The nauseous draughts, the blood-letting and blisters, have given place to moderate medication, the choice of climate and the regulation of diet. Women have been admitted as copartners with men in the guardianship of the public health. Athletic sports help the student to fresh blood and efficient muscle, without which the brain sickens and perishes.

But even in this department how much is left to desire and to do! Our greatest and richest city is still festering with the corruption that breeds disease. No board of health seems to have power to sweep its side streets and dark alleys. Fashion keeps her avenues clean, and neglects the rest of the vast domain, for which she has her reward in many a ghastly epidemic. The late Edward Clarke, of Boston, — heaven rest his soul! — could alarm the whole continent with his threats of the physical evils which the more perfect education of one sex would entail on both. But he has left no public protest against the monstrosities of toilet which deform and mutilate the bodies of women to-day, nor against the selfish frivolity of life in both sexes, which is equally inimical to true motherhood and to true fatherhood.

I have seen in fashions of dress and furniture the curious cycle which my elders foretold, and which it takes, I should think, half a century to fulfil. My earliest childish remembrance is of the slim dresses which display as much as is possible of the outlines of the figure. I remember the *élégantes* of Gotham walking the one fashionable street of fifty-five years ago, attired in pelisses of pink or blue satin. A white satin cloak trimmed with dark fur seemed, even to my childish observation, a chill costume for a pedestrian in the heart of winter. My mother's last Paris bonnet, bought probably in 1825, appeared to her children, twenty years later, such a caricature, that pious hands destroyed it, in order that we might have no ludicrous association with the sweet young creature whose death had left us babes in the nursery.

After many fluctuations and oscillations, I have seen modern head-gear near of kin to the subject of this holocaust. I have seen the old forms and colors return to popular favor. I have even heard that the very white satin cloak, which seemed *outré* to the critic of six years, has been worn and greatly admired in the recent gay world of Paris.

The return in these cases, it must be said, is not to the identical point of departure. Progress, according to some thinkers, follows a spiral, and is neither shut in a circle nor extended in a straight line. The hoops of our great-grand-mothers are not the hoops which we remember to have seen or worn. Their eelskin dresses are not the model of ours. Still, the recurrence of the same vein of fancy marks a periodical approxima-tion to the region or belt of influence in which certain forgotten possibilities suggest themselves to the seeker of novelty, and in which the capri-cious, antithetical fancy delights to crown with honor all that it found most devoid of beauty a few lustres ago.

Does this encyclical tendency in the familiar æsthetics of life imply a corresponding tendency in the moral and intellectual movement of man-kind? I fear that it does. I fear that serious-ness and frivolity, greed and disinterest, extrav-agance and economy, in so far as these are social and sympathetic phenomena, do succeed each other in the movement of the ages. But here the device of the spiral can save us. We must make the round, but we may make it with an up-ward inclination. "Let there be light!" is sometimes said in accents so emphatic, that the universe remembers and cannot forget it. We carry our problem slowly forward. With all the ups and downs of every age, humanity constantly rises. Individuals may preserve all its early delusions, commit all its primitive crimes ; but to the body of civilized mankind, the return to barbarism is impossible.

The æsthetic elaboration of ethical ideas, always a feature of civilization, becomes in our day a task of such prominence as to engage the zeal and labor of those even who have little natural facility for any of its processes.

The ignoring of this department of culture by our Puritan ancestors, had much to do with the bareness of surrounding and poverty of amusement which almost affright us in the record of their society. With all their insufficiency, these periods of severe simplicity are of great importance in the history of a people. The temporary withdrawal from the sensible and pleasurable to the severe verities of ethical study accumulates a reserve force which is sure to be very precious in the emergencies to which all nations are exposed. The reaction against the extreme of this is as likely to be excessive as was the action itself.

If we tend to any extreme, nowadays, it is to that of making art take the place of thought, as may somewhat appear in the general rage for illustration and decoration.

The ministrations of art to ethics are indeed unspeakably grand and helpful. The cathedrals of the Old World, and its rich and varied galleries, preserve for us the fresh and naïve spirit of mediæval piety. Religious art, indeed, becomes almost secularized by its repetitions; yet each of its great works has the isolation of its own atmosphere, and speaks its own language, which we reverently learn while we look upon it.

Of all arts, music is the one most intimately interwoven with the ethical consciousness of our own time. The oratorios of Handel and of Mendelssohn so blend the sacred text and the divine music, that we think of the two together, and almost as of things so wedded by God, that man must not seek to put them asunder. When I have sat to sing in the chorus of the Messiah, and have heard the tenor take up the sweet burden of " Comfort ye my people!" I have felt the whole chain of divine consolation which those historic words express, and which link the prophet of pre-Christian times to the saints and sinners of to-day.

In far-off Palestine I have been shown the plain
on which it is supposed that the shepherds were
tending their flocks when the birth of the Messiah was announced to them. But as I turned my
eyes to view it, my memory was full of that pasto-
ral symphony of Handel's, in which the divine
glory seems just muffled enough to be intelligible
to our abrupt and hasty sense. Nay, I lately
heard a beloved voice which read the chapter of
Elijah's wonderful experiences in the wilderness. ·
While I listened, bar after bar of Mendelssohn's
music struck itself off in the resonant chamber of
memory, and I thanked the Hebrew of our own
time for giving the intensity of life to that mysti-
cal drama of insight and heroism.

The transcendentalists of our own country
made great account of the relation of art to ethics,
and perhaps avenged the Puritan partiality by giving art the leading, and ethics the subordinate
place in their statements and endeavors. But
the masters of the transcendental philosophy in
Europe did not so. Spinoza, Kant, and Fichte
were idealists of the severest type. Standing for
the moment between the two, I will only say that
the danger of forgetting the high labors and re-
wards of thought in the pleasure of beautiful

sights and sounds is one to which the highest civilization stands most exposed. To think aright,
to resolve and pray aright, we must retire from
those delights to the contemplation of that whose
sublimity they can but faintly image, as we pass with
joy from the likeness of our friend into his presence.

Love of ornament is by no means synonymous
with love of the beautiful. The taste which over-
loads dress and architecture with superflous irrel-
evancies, is often quite in opposition to that true
sense of beauty which is indispensable to the artist
and precious to the philosopher. " *To καλόν*," the
Greeks said. Was it a naïve utterance on their
part? Was it through their poverty of expression, or their want of experience, that the same
word with them signified the good and the beautiful? No. It was through the depth of their insight, and the power of their mental appreciation,
that they so stamped this golden word as that it
should show the supreme of form on one of its
faces, and the supreme of spirit on the other.

The social domain of religion has also undergone a change. In my early life I remember
that all earnest and religious people were supposed to live out of the great world, and to keep
company only with one another and with the sub-

jects of their charitable beneficence. The disad-
vantages of this course are easily seen. Free
intercourse with the average of mankind is one
of the most important agencies in enlarging and
correcting the action of the human mind. The
exigencies of ordinary intercourse develop a sense
of the dependence of human beings upon each
other, and a power corresponding to the needs in-
volved in this interdependence. The religious
susceptibilities of individuals, which are at once
very strong in their character and very uncer-
tain in their action, are liable to become either
exaggerated or exhausted by a course of life which
should rely wholly upon them for guidance and
for interest.

Let us, therefore, by all means have saints in
the world, keeping to their pure standard, and
recommending it more by their actions than by
their professions. But these saints must be brave
as well as pure. Unworthy doctrine must not
escape their reprobation. When a just cause is
contemned, they must stand by it. If the world
shall cast them out in consequence, it will not be
their fault. The social leagues which group themselves around the various churches of to-day,
seem to me a feature of happy augury. It is the

office of the church to inspire and direct the tone of social intercourse, and these associations should greatly help it to that end. I lately heard Wendell Phillips complain that church exercises nowadays largely consist of picnics and other merry-makings. Only a little before, Mr. Phillips, in his reply to Mr. Parkman's article against Woman Suffrage, had spoken of the growth of social influence as a good.

It does, to be sure, look a little whimsical to read on the bulletin of a Methodist church such announcements as this, — " Private theatricals for the benefit of the Sunday school." But Wesley introduced the use of secular tunes in his church on the ground that the devil should not have all the good music. Neither should he monopolize the innocent amusements with which, if they are left to him, he does indeed play the devil.

Although the great ocean will always hold Europe at arm's length from us, yet the currents of belief and sympathy bring its various peoples near to us in various ways. I remember to have taken note of this long before the ocean steamships brought the eastern hemisphere within a few days' journey from our own seaboard, and very long before the time-annihilating cables were dreamed of. The

French have always had with us the prestige of their social tact and sumptuary elegance. The English manners are affected by those among us who mistake the aristocracy of position for the aristocracy of character. The Italians rule us by their great artists in the past, and by their subtle policy in the present. The Germans have, as they deserve, the pre-eminence in music, in metaphysics, and in many departments of high culture.

I have not long since been taken to task by a writer in a prominent New York paper for some strictures regarding the quasi-omnipotence of money in the society of to-day. The writer in question enlarged somewhat upon the greatly increased expenditure of money in our own country, as if this must be considered as a good in itself. He concludes his statement by remarking that Mrs. Howe has never studied the proper significance of the money question. I desire to say here only that I have not neglected the study of this question, which so regards the very life of society. One of its problems I have ventured to decide for myself, viz., whether the luxury of the rich really supports the industry of the poor.

The æsthetic of luxury is a mean and superficial

one. The critique of luxury is compliant and cowardly ; and, despite its glittering promise to pay any price for what it desires, luxury orders poorly, pays poorly, and in the end undermines the credit of the State, the very citadel of its solvency. I regret and deplore its prevalence to-day, and consider it not as the safeguard, but as the most dangerous enemy of republican institutions.

In our America, ay, even in our Puritan New England, the day has come in which economy is a discredit and poverty a disgrace. With the common school ever at work to lift the social level, unfolding to the child of the day-laborer the page which instructs the son of the peer, the cry is still that money is God, and that there is none other. One may ask, in the business streets, whether rich people have any faults, or poor people any virtues. A woman who sells her beauty for a rich dower is honored in church and in State. Both alike bow to the money in her hand. One proverb says that Time is money, as if it were

"Only that, and nothing more." •

Another proverb says that Money is power. And in this form, no doubt, it receives the most fervent worship, for luxury palls sooner or later, while ambition is never satisfied. But we constantly meet, on the other hand, with instances in which money is not power. Money does not give talent or intelligence. You cannot buy good government, good manners, or good taste. You cannot buy health or life. Do some of you remember the shipwreck, some twenty years ago, of a steamer homeward-bound from California? The few survivors told how the desperate passengers brought their belts and bags of gold to the cabin, and threw them about with a bitter contempt of their worthlessness. States have such shipwrecks, in which avenging Fate seems to say to those who have sacrificed all for wealth, "Thy money perish with thee."

The heroics of history are full of the story of great ends, accomplished by very small means. Now a handful of resolute men hold the forces of a great empire in check, and beat back the ocean surge of barbarism from the marble of their strong will. Now a single martyr turns the scale of the world's affection by throwing into the balance the weight of one small life. Now a State with every disadvantage of territory, cursed with sterility, or exposed to the murderous overflow of the salt sea, takes its stand upon the simple determination to conquer for itself a free and worthy existence. Frederick of Prussia and his small army, Washington, with his handful of men, in these and so many other instances, we admire the attainment of mighty ends through means which seem infinitesimal in proportion to them. How shall it be in our country, to which Nature has given the widest variety of climate, soil, and production? Shall we become a lesson to the world in the opposite direction? Shall we show how little a people may accomplish with every circumstance in its favor, and with nothing wanting to its success but the careful mind and resolute spirit? God forbid!

The belief in pacific methods of settling international differences has made a noticeable progress in my time.

In my school-days I remember a grave Presbyterian household at whose fireside I one day saw an elderly man seat himself, with little notice from the members of the family. I inquired who he might be, and was told, with some good-natured laughter, that this old gentleman was the American Peace Society, *i. e.*, the last surviving member of that association. This was a humorous exaggeration of the truth. Judge Jay, of New

York, was living at that time, and all the enthusiasm of the peace cause lived in him, and no
doubt in many others. I have remembered the
incident, nevertheless; and when I have seen the
stately Peace Congresses held in Europe and elsewhere, when I have seen rapacious England sub-
mitting to arbitration, when I have seen the flag
of military prestige go down before the white
banner of Peace, as in the late change of the
ministry in that country, I have remembered that
day of small things, and have learned that the
faith of individuals is the small seed from which
spring the mighty growths of popular conviction
and sympathy.

The extensive wars which have taken place
within the last forty years, as extensive and as
deadly as any the world ever saw, are sometimes
quoted in derision of those who believe, as I do, in
the sober, steady growth of the pacific spirit
among people of intelligence. The reasons for
this advance lie deeper than the vision of the
careless observer may reach. Within the period
of our own century the value of human life to the
individual has been greatly increased by the wide
diffusion of the advantages of civilization. The
value of the individual to the State has become

greatly increased by the multiplication of indus-
trial resources, and by the immense emigration
which at times threatens to drain the older society
of its working population. The spread of education has at once undermined the blind belief of
the multitude in military leaders, and toned down
the blind ferocity of instinct to which those leaders
are forced to appeal. Wars of mere spoliation are
scarcely permitted to-day. Wars of pure offence
are deeply disapproved of.

The military and diplomatic injustice of past
times has left unsettled many questions of territory and boundary which will not rest until they
shall be set right. The populations which war
has plundered and subjugated, lay their cause
before the world's tribunal. In aid of this, the
friends of the true law and order are ever busy in
forming a nucleus of moral power, which govern-
ments will be forced to respect. Thus, though
the war-demon dies hard, he is doomed, and we
shall yet see the battlements of his grim cathedrals places for lovers to woo and for babes to
play in.

In religion I have seen the dark ministrations
of terror give way before the radiant gospel of
hope. I remember when Doctrine sat beside the

bed of death, and offered its flimsy synonym to
the eyes upon which the awful, eternal truth was
about to dawn.   I remember when a man with a
poor diploma and a human commission assumed
to hold the keys of heaven and hell in his hands,
and to dispense to those who would listen to him
such immortality as he thought fit.   I remember
when it went hard with those who, in forming
their religious opinions, persisted in daring to use
the critical power of their own judgment.   They
were lonely saints; they wandered in highways and
byways, unrecognized, excommunicated of men.
No one had power to burn their bodies, but it was
hoped that their souls would not escape the tor-
ment of eternal flame.   I have seen this time, and
I have lived to see a time in which these rejected
stones, hewn and polished by God's hand, have
come to be recognized as corner-stones in the prac-
tical religious building of the age.   What a discredit was it once to hear Theodore Parker !   How
happy are they now esteemed who have heard him !
Let not Mr. Emerson's urbanity lead him to forget
the days in which polite Boston laughed him to
scorn.   Brook Farm was once looked upon as a
most amusing caricature.   But when the world
learned something about Nathaniel Hawthorne,

George Ripley, William Henry Channing, John Dwight, and George William Curtis, the public heart bowed itself with remorseful homage before the ruined threshold of what was, with all its short-comings, a blameless temple to ideal humanity.

It is quite true that every change which I have seen in the society of my time cannot be said to be, in itself, for the better. The price of progress, like that of liberty, is eternal vigilance.

A time of religious enfranchisement may induce a period of religious indifference. Cosmopolitan enlargement may weaken the force of patriotism. The charity of society may degenerate into an indifference concerning private morals, which, if it could prevail, would go far towards destroying public ones. Humanity ever needs the watchman on the tower. It needs the warning against danger, the guidance out of it. I can imagine a set of prophets less absolute than the Hebrew seers, whose denunciation of evils, near or present, should always couple itself with profound and sober suggestions of help. And this will be the work of faith in our day, to believe in the good which can overcome the evil, and to seek it with earnest and brave persistence.

Let me return for a moment, very briefly, to

what I touched upon just now, the great changes in religious thought which this century has witnessed. What manifold contrasts have we observed in this domain! What a wild and wide chase in the fields of·conjecture! What impatience with the idols of the past, historical and metaphysical! There have been moments in the last twenty years in which one might have said to the religious ideals of past ages that the time had come in which every one who raised his hand against them thought that he was doing God service. This iconoclasm had its time, and, one supposes, its office.

But the religious necessities of mankind are permanent, and will outlast any and all systems of pure criticism. The question arises, in all this havoc of illusory impressions, Who is to provide for the culture and direction of those instincts of reverence which are so precious to, so ineradicable in the race? We must ask this service of those who believe that religion is, on the whole, wiser than its critics. Those who have been able to hold fast this persuasion will be the religous trainers of our youth. Those who have relinquished it will have no more skill to teach religion than a sculptor will have to feed an army.

The greatest trouble with human society is, that

its natural tendency leads it, not to learn right measure through one excess, but, on becoming convinced of this, to rush into an opposite excess with equal zeal and equal error. The mechanism of society requires constant correction in order to keep up the succession of order and progress through and despite this proneness to extravagance and loss of power. This rectification of direction without interruption of movement is the office of critical and constructive thought. Precious are the men, and rare as precious, who carry this balance in their minds, and, while the ship lurches now on this side and now on that, strain after the compass with masterful courage and patience. We have all known such men, but we have known, too, that their type is not a common one.

Among all who are out of work to-day, so far as the market is concerned, those men of careful and critical judgment are the least called for, and the least wished for by the majority of men. Headlong enthusiasm, headlong activity, headlong doubt and cynicism, the prevalence of these shows the force with which the present whirl of the spindle was cast. Fair and softly, my quick-flying Century. To find out whether you are going right or

wrong, whether you are faithful or faithless, sol
vent or bankrupt, you must have recourse to these
same slow, patient men and women, who try such
questions by a more accurate and difficult method
than that of the popular inclination.

I find that the philosopher Kant, writing more
than a hundred years ago, remarks that in so
sociable an age as his own Culture must naturally
be expected to assume an encyclopedic character.
It will, he says, necessarily desire to present a
manifold number of agreeable and instructive
acquisitions, easy of apprehension, for entertainment in friendly intercourse.

These words seem prophetic of the efforts after
general information, with a view to conversation
as an accomplishment, which have constituted a
marked feature of American and English society
within forty years.   In the dissolving view of the
public predilection, this object has lost much of its
prominence.   The ornate and well-rounded periods
of the conversationist are not more in request, nowadays, than were the high-sounding sentiments of
Joseph Surface to Sir Peter Teazle, when experience had shown him their emptiness.

Blunt speech and curt expression rather are in
favor.   The heroines of novels are supposed to

fall in love with men of a somewhat brutal type. Adonis is out of fashion. Hercules pleases, and even Vulcan is preferred. One thinks that the influence of the mercantile spirit may be recognized in this change. Long speeches and roundabout statements are found not to pay. The man who listens to them with one ear, hearkens with the other for the ocean telegrams, news of the stock market, considers the maturing of a note, the success or failure of a scheme. When there is no one to listen, loquacity itself will grow economical of breath.

The world is quite right in its tacit protest against over talk. A great deal of empty, irrelevant speech is liable to be imposed upon the good-nature of society in the garb of instructive conversation. It is weary to listen by the hour to men or women who principally teach you their own opinion of their own erudition. But woe to the world if its haste and greed should ever be such that the true teacher should want an audience, the long lessons of philosophy find interpreters, but no pupils.

The present is, on the whole, an encyclopedic, cosmopolitan era. I suppose that it succeeds as a reaction to one of more special and isolated endeavor. The example and influence of Goethe have had much to do with the formation of the ideas of culture which have been prevalent in our time. This wonderful man went, with such a happy tact, from one thing to another. In poetry he did so much, in high criticism so much, in science so much, and in world-wisdom so much! How naturally were the lovers of study, who made him their model, led to undertake, as he did, to render the most eminent service, to attain the highest honors in a dozen different departments!

But the man Goethe was more wonderful even than his writings. His individuality was too powerful to suffer loss through the variety of his pursuits. He could be at once a courtier and a philosopher, a poet and a scientist, a critic of morals and a man of the world, and in all things remain himself.

I sometimes wonder why we Americans are so apt to show, in our conduct and remarks, an undue preponderance of what the phrenologists term love of approbation. This is an amiable and useful trait in human nature, which may degenerate into a weak and cowardly vanity, or even into a malignant selfishness. To desire the approbation which can enlighten us as to the merits of what we have done or attempted, is wise as well as graceful. To make constant laudation a prominent object in any life is a capital mistake in its ordering. To prefer the praise of men to the justification of conscience, is at once cowardly and criminal. I observe these three phases in American life. I value the first, compassionate the second, and reprobate the third. Surely, if there is any virtue which a republican people is bound to show, it is that self-respect which is the only true majesty, and which can afford to be as generous and gracious as majesty should be.

It is, perhaps, natural that many of us should, through a want of experience, mistake the standpoint of people conspicuous in the older European society as greatly superior to our own. We can learn much, indeed, from the observation of such a standpoint; but, in order to do so, we must hold fast our own plain, honest judgment, as we derive it from education, inheritance, and natural ability.

It must, I should think, be very tedious and very surprising to Europeans to hear Americans complain of being so young, so crude, so immature. This is not according to nature. Imagine a nursery full of babies who should bewail the

fact of their infancy. Any one who should hear
such a complaint would cry out, "Why, that's
the best thing about you. You have the new-
ness, the promise, the unwasted vigor of child-
hood, — gifts so great that Christ enjoined it upon
holy men to recover, if they had lost them."

If our society is young, its motto should be the
saying of Saint Paul to Timothy, "Let no man
despise thy youth." The great men of our early
history deserve to rank with the ripest products
of civilization. Was Washington crude? Was
Franklin raw? Were Jay, Jefferson, and Hamil-
ton immature? The authorities of the older
world bowed down to them, and did them homage. The Republicans of France laid the key of
the Bastille at the feet of Washington. Franklin was honored and admired in the court circle
of Louis XVI. There was a twofold reason for
this. These men represented the power and vigor
of our youth; but our youth itself represented
the eternal principles of truth and justice, for
whose application the world had waited long.
And thinking people saw in us the dignity of
that right upon which we had founded our hope
and belief as a nation.

I will instance a single event of which I heard

much during my last visit in Rome. A German, naturalized in America, and who had made a large fortune by a railroad contract in South America, had purchased from some European government the title of "Count." He was betrothed to the sister-in-law of a well-known California millionnaire, whose wife has been for some years a resident of Paris, where her silver, her diamonds, and her costly entertainments are matters of general remark. All of these parties are Roman Catholics. The wedding took place in Rome, and was signalized by a festival, at which twelve horses, belong to the bridegroom, were ridden in a race, whose prizes were bestowed by the hand of the bride. The invitations for this occasion were largely distributed by a monsignor of the Romish Church, and the king of Italy honored the newly married pair by his presence.

Not long after this, I read in the Italian papers that this very count had become a candidate for a seat in the Italian Parliament. I suppose that money will assist an election as much in Italy as elsewhere. The monsignor who interested himself so efficiently about the invitations for the wedding party, was none other than the master of ceremonies of Pope Leo XIII. He would, no doubt, have taken even greater interest in the return of his friend to the Parliament. I do not know whether this gentleman has ever succeeded in usurping the place of a representative of the Italian people; but the chance of his being able to do so lay in the American gold of which he had become possessed. Here is one instance of the direct relations between Rome and America which Americans so placidly overlook.

In this day of the world hope is so strong, and the desire for an improved condition so prevalent, that much may be looked for in Europe as the result of the legitimate. action and influence of America. But if American capital busies itself with upholding the shams of the old world, if American taste and talent are led and pledged to work with the reactionary agents everywhere against the enfranchisement of the human race, where shall the hope of the world find refuge?

Goldsmith has a touching picture of the emigrants who, in his time, were compelled to leave the country which would not feed them, for a distant bourne, which could, by no means, be to them a home. But let us assist at the embarkation of another group of exiles. These people have been living abroad, and are about to return home. The rich, beautiful land whose discovery has changed the fortunes of the human race, invites them on the other side of the Atlantic. The flag which represents the noblest chapter of modern history waves over them.

From dynastic, aristocratic Europe they go to inherit the work of an ancestry heroic in thought and action. They go to the land which still boasts a Longfellow, a Whittier, an Emerson, a Harriet Beecher Stowe. Are they glad? Are they happy? No. They have learned the follies of the old world, not its wisdom. They are not going home,—they are going into exile.

Let us look a little at their record in the Europe which they regret so passionately. They went abroad with money, and the education which it commands, with leisure and health. What good deeds may they not have done! What gratifying remembrance may they have left behind them!. Shall we not find them recorded as donors to many a noble charity, as students in many a lofty school? We shall indeed, sometimes. But in many cases we shall hear only of their fine clothes and expensive entertainments, with possible mortifying anecdotes of their fast behavior.

If the mother leaves a daughter behind her, it

6

is likely to be as the wife of some needy European nobleman, who despises all that she is bound to hold dear, and is proud not to know that which it should be her glory to understand.

I said at Concord, and I say it to-day, that the press is much affected by the money debauch of the period. Let us examine the way in which this result is likely to be brought about.

A newspaper or periodical is almost always an investment in which the idea of gain is very prominent. This expectation may either regard what the proposed paper shall earn as a medium of information, or the profit of certain enterprises which its statements may actively promote.

Special organs are founded for special emergencies, as is a campaign sheet, or for the advocate of special reforms, like the antislavery "Standard" of old, and the "Woman's Journal" of to-day. These papers rarely repay either the money advanced for them, or the literary labor bestowed upon them.

Under the head of its earnings the newspaper depends upon two classes of persons, viz., its advertisers and its subscribers. Either or both of these may be displeased by the emphatic mention of some certain fact, the expression of some certain opinion. "If we tell this unwelcome truth," say the managers, "we shall lose such and such subscribers. If we take this stand, some of our wealthiest advertising firms will choose another medium of communicating with the public." The other set of considerations just spoken of, the enterprises which are to be favored and promoted, may still more seriously affect the tone and action of the paper, which will thus be drawn in a twofold way to lend itself to the publication only of what it will pay to say.

The annals of journalism in this country will, no doubt, show a fair average of courageous and conscientious men among its chiefs. I am willing to believe all things and to hope all things in this direction. But I must confess that I fear all things, too, in view of a great power, whose position makes it almost an irresponsible one. And I should regard with great favor the formation of an unofficial censorship of public organs, in view not so much of what may be published, as of what is unfairly left out of the statements and counterstatements of conflicting interests.

Of all the changes which I can chronicle as of my own time, the change in the position of women is perhaps the most marked and the least anticipated by the world at large. Whatever opinions heroic men and women may have held concerning this from Plato's time to our own, the most enlightened periods of history have hardly given room to hope that the sex in general would ever reach the enfranchisement which it enjoys to-day. I date the assurance of its freedom from the hour in which the first university received women graduates upon the terms accorded to pupils of the opposite sex. For education keeps the key of life, and a liberal education insures the first conditions of freedom, viz., adequate knowledge and accustomed thought. This first and greatest step gained, the gate of professional knowledge and experience quickly opened, and that of political enfranchisement stands already ajar. The battle can have but one result, and it has been fought, with chivalrous temper and determination, not by one sex against the other, but by the very gospel of fairness and justice against the intrenched might of selfish passion, inertia, and prejudice. Equal conditions of life will lift the whole level of society, which is so entirely one body that the lifting or lowering of one half lifts or lowers the other half. This change, which in the end appeared to come suddenly, has been prepared by such gradual ten-

tatives, by such long and sound labor, that we need
not fear to lose sight of it in any sudden collapse.
There are women of my age, and women of earlier
generations, who have borne it in their hearts all
their lives through, who have prayed and worked
for it, without rest and without discouragement.
Horace Mann was its apostle, Theodore Parker was
its prophet, Margaret Fuller, Lucy Stone, and a
host of wise and true-hearted women, whom the
time would fail me to name, have been its female
saints. It was in nature; they have brought it
into life; even as Christ said, "My Father work-
eth hitherto, and I work." The slender thread
which crossed the dark abyss of difficulty was not
the silken spinning of vanity, nor the cobweb fibre
of madness. From the faith of pure hearts the
steadfast links were wrought, and the great chasm
is spanned, and is ready to become the strong and
sure highway of hope, for this nation and for the
nations of the earth.

The customs of society prescribe the mental
garb and gait proper to those who desire the favor-
able notice of their peers in their own time. As
these are partly matters of tradition and inheritance, we can learn something of the merits and
demerits of a generation by studying the habits of

familiar judgment which it hands down to its successor. A narrow, ill-educated generation leaves behind it corresponding garments of rule and prescription, to which the next generation must for a time accommodate itself, because a custom or a fashion is not made in a day. The rulers of society seem often more occupied in dwarfing the mind to suit the custom than in enlarging the custom so as to fit it to the growth of mind. The most dangerous rebellions, individual and social, are natural revolts aginst the small tyranny which perpetuates the insufficiency of the past.

The copper shoes which so cramp the foot of a female infant in China as to destroy its power of growth, are not more cruel or deleterious than are the habits of unreflecting prejudice which compress the growth of human minds until they, too, lose their native power of expansion, and the idol Prejudice is enthroned and worshipped by those on whom it has imposed its own deformity as the standard of truth and beauty.

The heavy tasks which nature imposes upon women leave them less at leisure than men to reform and readjust these inherited garments. The necessity for prompt and early action obliges them to follow the intuitive faculties, as all must do who have not time to work out the problems of the reasoning ones. The instinct of possession is a ruling one in human nature, and a woman inheriting a superstition or a prejudice holds fast to it because it is something, and she has got it. It seems to her a possession. It may be a mischievous and unfortunate one, but it will take a good deal of time and thought to find that out. Those who have the training of women's minds often train them away from such a use of time and from such a labor of thought. Hence the fatal persistence of large classes of women in superstitions which the thinking world has outgrown, and the equally fatal zeal with which they impose the same insufficient modes of judgment upon their children.

I pray this generation of women, which has seen such enlargements of the old narrow order regarding the sex, I pray it to deserve its high post as guardian of the future. Let it bequeath to its posterity a noble standard of womanhood, free, pure, and, above all, laborious.

The standard of manhood really derives from that of womanhood, and not *vice versa*, as many imagine. However we may receive from tradition the order of their material creation, in that of training and education, the woman's influence comes before that of the man, and outlasts it.

The figure of the infant Christ dwells always in our mind, accompanied by that of the gracious mother who gave Him to the world.   Let the fact of this great gift prefigure to us the august office of Woman.   Hers be it also to preserve and transmit from age to age the Christian doctrine and the Christlike faith.   And, in order that she may fully realize the glory and blessedness of giving, let her remember that what is worthily given to one time is given to all time.